T0199222

LIFE AS I KNEW IT

Overcoming an Abusive Childhood

KARA REDKIN

authorHOUSE®

AuthorHouse™
1663 Liberty Drive
Bloomington, IN 47403
www.authorhouse.com
Phone: 1 (800) 839-8640

Published by AuthorHouse   08/14/2015

ISBN: 978-1-5049-2877-9 (sc)
ISBN: 978-1-5049-2876-2 (e)

Library of Congress Control Number: 2015912924

Print information available on the last page.

Any people depicted in stock imagery provided by Thinkstock are models,
and such images are being used for illustrative purposes only.
Certain stock imagery © Thinkstock.

This book is printed on acid-free paper.

Because of the dynamic nature of the Internet, any web addresses or links contained in
this book may have changed since publication and may no longer be valid. The views
expressed in this work are solely those of the author and do not necessarily reflect the
views of the publisher, and the publisher hereby disclaims any responsibility for them.

CHAPTER 1

My mother told me not to write this book until she was dead. As she ages, I begin to understand why. In her late 80's her mind is as sharp as ever; continuing to do research for her many books. I have no wish to remind her of unpleasant times, and so I write this in anticipation of her inevitable passing.

I have few happy memories of my childhood. Looking back, I am happy that Dad never went out to bars, or even drank. So it is even more perplexing to me that he was such a fierce and dreaded dad. One thing I'll say for Dad, he loved to read. I can imagine it was his way of escaping the realities of having to discipline four unruly kids.

By the time I came along, it was just the three of us girls. We were fairly noisy, and Dad had a night job. I suppose it was hard for him to sleep during the day when we were young. But this is how my Mom and Dad handled us kids. Mom worked days while Dad took care of us and I guess he slept while we napped.

My earliest memory of being with Dad while Nina and Anna were at school, is going to the hardware store with him. I remember him smiling a lot, really beaming with pride as he introduced me to his friend who owned the store. I must have been four at the time since I wasn't in school yet.

The day before Kindergarten was to start, I remember it was a bright, sunny day. Two weeks before I had just turned five and I comprehended little that was going on. My Mom had taught us all to read before we started school. She was a writer and knew the importance of such a head start.

My Dad parked his car at the school parking lot. The outside door to the classroom was propped wide open since it was such a sunny day, and we walked right in. It was "Meet The Teacher" day, and every child had an hour to familiarize themselves with the teacher and the classroom. My teacher, Mrs. Meyers, and my father talked while I played with the various toys. I remember a big wooden shoe that laced up for practice in tying a bow. When I got home I asked Dad to show me how to tie my shoe. It wasn't hard, it just required a lot of practice on my part. My little fingers had never had to maneuver in such an intricate way. I was so proud when I was not only able to duplicate the act, but was able to do it tightly, so it wouldn't come unraveled. No double-knotting here.

The next day was truly my first day of school and I was so excited. Too bad I missed it entirely. It just happened to be raining while my Dad drove me to school. He handed me milk money, and I said, "How many monies is this?"

"Two cents," he said.

I said, "Wow."

He didn't park this time, but told me he would let me off here at the roundabout, and pick me up after school in the same place. This was different. I looked at the door to the classroom. It was closed. At home Nina and Anna had told me, with fear in their voices, *never* to open a closed door. I had no idea that this only applied to my parent's bedroom when they were both inside. Apparently, Nina had once opened their door to be greeted with much shouting and running and spanking. So as a result, none of us ventured to open a closed door.

There was no way that my father could have known about this conspiratorial conversation between sisters, nor was I articulate enough to relay it to him. Instead, when I got out of the car, into the rain, I grabbed the no-parking pole and went around and around, determined to wait until that door was opened.

Well, that was apparently too much for my Dad. He got out of the car. At first I thought he was going to open the school door for me. But I was so wrong. He threw me back into the car and raced home. I had no idea what I was in for. But soon enough I found out. My Dad tore off my clothes, and I mean all of them. He took off his belt and went to town on my bare skin. I was so bruised there was no way I could make an appearance at school that day. So I missed my first day of school.

The second day of school went fine until the end when one of my class mates asked if I wanted to go home with her. I said, "Okay." We played at her house until her mother said it was time for me to go home. Well, I didn't exactly know how to get home from her house, only from school. So I wandered around a bit until I decided to knock on someone's door.

"Are you a lost little girl?" said the nice older woman.

"Yes. I can't find my way home," I said.

Well, she was used to this, living so close to the school. "Would you like some hot chocolate?"

"Yes, I would," I said.

"What is your father's name?" she inquired.

"Daddy," I replied.

"What is your last name?" she asked.

"I don't know."

"Don't worry, I know just what to do." She then called the police to report a missing girl.

"Does she have short blond hair and freckles?" asked the dispatcher.

"How on earth did you know that?" the woman replied.

"We've had a report of just such a little girl who went missing on her way home from school. Is her name Kara?"

"Yes. Oh, thank goodness," she said. She gave the dispatch her address and told me everything would be fine, that my daddy would be coming to get me.

I was so happy. I would be home soon, playing with my toys and watching TV. Little did I realize I was about to experience another, more horrendous display of my father's unrelenting anger.

As soon as I got into my Dad's car, he back-handed me across the face. Nothing could have prepared me for such stinging pain. Even the belt whipping from yesterday was forgotten. Looking back on it now, I tell myself that he trained our dog with much more patience than he had for my innocent behavior.

The weekend had arrived and our Mom was taking us to the lake, which was close to her mother's house. We spent many glorious days at my grandmother's house. She cooked from scratch and even taught me how to make a cherry pie with a lattice crust. She would send us to the corner store for milk or eggs, or whatever she needed for the dinner. All three of us, Nina, Anna and I, went and we each carried a little bag for the few things she needed. When we got back, we each received a quarter! We were so happy!

The next day we came back home with horrific sunburns from our lake activities. Our tender shoulders were blistered and every exposed limb was lobster-red. My Mom always said a nice warm bath helped everything. So she got all three of us in the tub. The warm water did help. We must have been quite noisy because all of a sudden, there was our Dad, yelling loudly. Meanwhile I reached for the soap.

He slapped me on my sunburned back and said, "Don't you *ever* turn your back when I'm talking to you!"

Well, I had no idea he was talking to *me*. I hadn't done anything wrong. I didn't understand. The slap stung me even more than the backhand did. When my Mom was toweling me off, I asked her, "Why did Daddy hurt my sunburn?"

She said, "I don't know, honey."

Looking back on it now, I hope he had heard that innocent exchange.

CHAPTER 2

We had a lot of fun at our Grandmother's house. One Christmas, I received a wonderful gift of underwear with the names of the weeks embroidered right on them. Another Christmas I got a Tressy doll whose hair could be pulled long or wound up short again inside her head. The most useful toy I ever received was a device with an alphabet dial built into it that allowed me to spell out a word that it "spoke." When I spelled the word correctly, it would reward me with "That's Correct!" I played with that until it broke, many months later. By then I knew how to spell all the many words in the toy. Of course by today's standards, it had a very small storage capacity. But it kept me quite busy and happy.

I was very inquisitive and always asked everyone how to spell this or that word. It was around the time of "Laugh-In" where the famous saying arose, "Look *that* up in your Funk and Wagnall!" And so for my 13th birthday that year I got a Funk & Wagnall paperback dictionary. I looked up everything in it that I didn't understand while reading my many library books. I was a voracious reader.

In the summer after sixth grade, I read *Gone With the Wind*. It was wonderful. I kept my dictionary handy for any "grown-up words" that I hadn't heard before. I was getting to be such a good speller, my mother got me a Washington Post Spelling Bee guide to prepare for taking my place in the National Spelling Bee in Washington, D.C. I was in the seventh grade when I tried out for the spelling bee's first elimination in a classroom at my school.

I sat at one of the desks and listened to the way the other students spelled their words. They started out with easy words. They were to stand up, say the word, then spell the word, and then say the word again. When it was my turn, I said, "Pillow. W-I-L-L-O-W. Pillow." Then I sat down and smiled. The teacher in charge told me that I could go now. I didn't understand. She explained that I just spelled Willow. I was so humiliated my face turned red before I was able to leave the classroom. I could hear the other students laughing. The teacher admonished them that there would be no laughing for mistakes.

When I got home I told everyone what had happened and they all laughed. Every once in a while someone in my family would ask me "How do you spell Pillow?" I would always answer, "W-i-l-l-o-w!" It was our favorite inside joke.

That summer my Mom bought a set of Encyclopedia Britannica. All summer long I would read, from A to Z, until I finished the entire series. I imagined all sorts of things I could accomplish. The only thing is, I didn't talk very much. It was my belief that if I but knew the Russian Alphabet, I could learn to read and write Russian. If only I had communicated this little known "fact" to someone who knew differently.

But I did learn French. All throughout my elementary years, as a group our classroom watched the local public educational network and learned French. Every year for an hour a day, from Kindergarten through the 6th grade we had a French lesson. This helped me enormously when it came to figuring out words from their French root. We didn't have any Latin classes, but French is a "romance" language, meaning that it has Latin roots. So when I learned that superior could also mean "upper," as in the head is superior to the neck, the word "supra" came to mind, which is Latin for "above." I use that word a lot now, working as a medical word processor.

One summer day I was sitting on the front porch, just chilling, when the mailman brought my Dad's Book of the Month Club selection. Having nothing to do, I opened the books and decided to read "Love Story". I finished it in a few days, and then handed it to my Dad and said, "I think you'll like this." He chuckled and said, "Thanks."

In 7th grade I took French. I thought I would get an easy "A" because of my elementary years of French. Well, the teacher gave me a "B" because I failed to turn in one assignment. I was pretty indignant and decided in the 8th grade I'd take Spanish. It was pretty easy for me to learn to read and write both French and Spanish, but for some reason I could never speak them very well. That's because as a child, I didn't talk very much. I kept my thoughts to myself and "talked to God."

We went to a Baptist Church and Sunday School, all except for my Dad. One day while walking to Church I asked why I had to go to church when Dad never went, and I got a spanking. Mom's spankings never really hurt, but were somewhat of a humiliation.

I had a paper route year-round early in the morning. Many times, while walking to each subscriber, I would say in my head, "God, please take me home." That was my plea to be allowed to go to Heaven. By 8th grade I had had enough of being given a bloody nose for every imagined wrong. If the house was messy when my Dad came home from work, he woke us all up in the middle of the night. After giving us all bloody noses, he would say, "Clean up this pig sty!" He knew just how to cup his hand to give us a "compression" nose bleed. The air forced into our nostrils would break the capillaries and give us bloody noses without any bruises. I will never forget that.

Nobody trained us up to be responsible children. Is it any wonder that we all left the house as soon as we possibly could? And that we all had babies by the time we were 19?

One day I was carrying a chair downstairs to my basement bedroom and I bumped my hip. My Mom asked me what was wrong. I mouthed off at her saying, "You don't care, why would you want to know?"

Well my Dad was hot on my trail and caught me up by the hair, slapping me left and right until I was in hysterics. Nina told me that was child abuse. That was the first time I had heard that term used in

CHAPTER 3

Steve was born six months after my sixth birthday. We girls all adored him. He was little more than 2 the first time he answered "No!" to my Dad. We were all in the living room when Dad told Steve to "come here." After he said "No" there was a collective audible intake of air through our mouths. Nobody ever said no to my Dad.

Dad was on his feet in seconds, snatching Steve up into the air and spanking the living daylights out of him. He never said "No" to my Dad again.

One day we were playing in the living room with Steve while my Mom was in the kitchen pouring coffee for a neighbor lady. We were telling Steve to do this or that just to see the little bugger run his little legs off in his cute little diapers. He was having a ball. One of us told him to get a napkin from the kitchen. He ran into the kitchen and saw a napkin on the kitchen counter that was directly underneath a just-poured cup of steaming coffee. He grabbed the napkin and the entire cup of coffee spilled on his leg, all the way down to his ankle. The blood-curdling scream was terrifying, even as I remember it today. His tender skin literally melted away from his leg. The ambulance came for him and he had to have plastic surgery. He had to stay in the burn unit for weeks before he was allowed to come home. Only my Mom visited him. My Dad didn't. Many nights we girls stayed in the hospital hallway while my Mom read to Steve. His favorite book was *Mike Mulligan and the Steam Shovel*. That had been my favorite too. My Mom read that book to him every night, repeatedly, until he went to sleep.

He gradually healed, but it was a slow process. I don't think my Mom was ever the same afterwards. She never invited anyone over again and none of us ever had anything to do with our neighbors. Until Susan Green moved across the street. She had a little girl just my age and we would play for hours in her back yard. She would always say "Let's pretend to …" And I would say, "Don't say let's pretend. Let's just do it." I think she was much more articulate than I was.

Sometimes I would watch her mother type on a little electric typewriter. She didn't look at the keys as she typed. I told my Mom that I wanted to learn to do that. So we bought a little electric typewriter with green stamps and my Dad bought me a text book to learn to type. I really loved learning to type. My Dad was proud of me. He just smiled as he listened to me typing faster with each lesson that I took. By the time I was in 8th grade, I was typing my Mom's books. One day my Dad took me to his work to do some typing for him. I was so happy when I was typing. It was so fun.

When I took an official typing course that summer I was way ahead of everyone else. During one typing test the teacher announced, "Type as fast as you possibly can, but endeavor to hit the right keys." I always liked that saying. After five minutes into the test, the teacher said, "Kara, you can stop now." I looked at her puzzled, and then looked at my paper which had already become filled up and was then on the floor. She said, "You passed the speed test. Now let me grade your accuracy." She handed my paper back to me without saying a word. She didn't want to discourage the other students. I typed 103 words per minute with 1 mistake.

After the class ended, the teacher told me, "Don't bother to take the advanced class." Instead I took Accounting for Business. The teacher was so interesting. She had been to Japan and always said, "Ichiban means Number One. Always strive to become Ichiban."

We learned the double-entry type of bookkeeping where you *credit* cash going out and then have to *debit* the account that the cash bought on behalf of, such as supplies. The teacher made the course very interesting, like we were sole proprietors of a small business. It was a lot of fun. When the class was over, she gave those of us that were receptive a kit and an instruction booklet that treated us like a real small business. I started it on my own, but soon found more to do with the rest of my summer, like going to the lake and reading books. But to this day I can whip up a spreadsheet on the computer to account for my income and all my "accounts" where my cash flow goes, with each of my accounts on a separate sheet of the spreadsheet.

CHAPTER 4

It was the summer of my junior year. My sister, Anna was a senior, and getting into lots of trouble. Nina was out of the house, going to college. In reality, Nina was secretly married and pregnant. But she was not in trouble. She was respectably married.

One day Anna was going to a party where she confided in me that she was going to try LSD. I told her she shouldn't. But she wanted to. My Dad actually drove her to the party. When he came back, I told him what Anna told me. I didn't want her to get into drugs. My Dad drove back to the party and drug her out of the house and back-handed her in the car.

Anna later said to me, "Why did you tell him?"

I told her, "I didn't want you to take LSD."

She said, "Do you know what it's like to be drug out of a party in front of all your friends by your Dad?"

I told her "Maybe you have the wrong kind of friends." They were obviously into drugs.

She didn't want to hear it.

Apparently she never listened to me because she kept getting into trouble with drugs. One day her friends literally dropped her off at home, rang the doorbell and ran off. Anna was drugged into a stupor.

My Dad kept yelling at her, "What did you take?" He knew how serious that kind of behavior could be. She could have died.

My parents were so tired of her behavior when my Mom and Anna and I took our last trip to the lake near our Grandmother's house. Anna got permission from my Mom to walk around near the shops. I stayed with my Mom at the shore. Even as a Junior I was pretty naïve and immature. A couple at the shore were making out pretty heavily, laying on a towel on the sand. The dude was actually on top of the girl.

I asked my Mom, "What are they doing?"

She said, "They shouldn't be doing that here. Don't watch."

She turned her back, but I couldn't help but watch. I was intrigued. I had never had a boyfriend and I was 16. I was an over-protected kid. But I didn't mind because I couldn't hold a conversation with anyone. I just had a total lack of social experience. I had a best friend all throughout elementary school, but ever since 7th grade, I was a loner.

When my sister came back from the shops, we went to our Grandmother's house. Little did we know that she had met a guy and had planned to meet up with him later. She was 17 and she thought she was an adult. She was always giving my Mom trouble. When my Mom spanked her, it had no effect on her. She just took it and kept a straight face. She did not give my Mom the satisfaction of crying after a spanking.

The next morning we were ready to leave my Grandmother's house and go home. But my Mom's car was not where she left it. Someone had stolen her car. And Anna was missing. It was deduced that since my Mom kept her keys in her purse, Anna must have stolen the car.

We had to get home. My Mom had to go to work the next day, so she rented a car. On the way back home, not too far from my Grandmother's house, my Mom spotted her car. My Mom honked her horn to get Anna's attention. When Anna realized it was Mom, she pulled into a parking lot and three people ran out of the car and they all went running in different directions. My sister pulled out of the parking lot and was determined to continue to run away with the car.

Anna came to a stop light with us right behind her. She was preparing to run the red light, entering a very busy freeway. My Mom had to stop her. She rammed the back of her own car with the rental car and both cars were suddenly out of commission. Anna was saved from certain death. My Mom went to a local store and called the police. The store owner took a hold of Anna, making sure she didn't get away. The police came quickly. They took Anna and put her in the police car, and then put her in a cell at the police station. My Mom drove us to the police station where we waited for my Dad. Anna was in for the worse beating of her life.

When my Dad came we all went into a large interrogation room. Anna was escorted in by the local police and they then left the room. The first thing my Dad did was hand-cuff Anna so she couldn't defend herself. He began screaming at her and beating her in the face. There was a little window in the door where the local police took turns watching. I wondered why they didn't put a stop to this beat-down. At one point my Dad hit my sister in the face so hard that his watch hit the opposite wall 50 feet away and smashed to pieces.

The ordeal took 30 minutes. Every time my Dad hit her, Anna would scream at him, saying, "I bet it makes you feel like a big man hitting a girl like that." This only made him angrier and cost her another beating. When it was all over, we were all headed to my Mom's car when my Dad told my sister, "Oh, no, you don't. You're coming with me!" The look on my sister's face was pathetically panicked. She actually thought our Dad was going to kill her on the way home. It is my guess that he got a few more smacks in before arriving home.

The next day a neighbor friend of Anna's came over and asked if she could come out. Anna didn't want anyone to know that she was bruised all over and told me to tell her that she was sick.

I refused. I told her friend that Anna couldn't come out because she has two black eyes that my Dad gave her. I told her everything that happened. I wasn't going to lie for my father any more. The family secret had to come out.

CHAPTER 5

It was just a matter of time. I met a guy. I was 17 and had been going to my local church youth group all summer. I never got into trouble anymore. I was driving and my Dad gave me a used car that he made sure was running right. A visitor to our youth group asked me for a ride home. He was living in a half-way house in nearby Springfield, MO. When I found a parking space, he invited me in. The house was filled with young people my age and older. A guy in the corner, George, was "holding court" telling a story to a large group of hangers-on. I was intrigued by how he kept his audience captivated. Since I never was able to hold a conversation for long, I was amazed that he could just go on and on and make people laugh. I eventually moved my way over so I could actually hear what he was saying. But that was when he noticed me and concluded his story so he could talk to me. He was a little full of himself, and I didn't have the heart to tell him that I hadn't heard one word of his story. He thought I was enthralled with him. I was just interested in his ability for public speech. I could never address such a group myself.

We went for a walk in the streets of Springfield, MO. He bought us sodas and we sat down and talked. We agreed to have a picnic the next day in the park. When he said goodbye to me he kissed me with his tongue in my mouth. I didn't know what I thought about that. I had never encountered that before. In fact, that was the first time I was kissed by a boy. It was April, and I was going to be 18 in August. We had all summer to get to know each other, I thought.

The next day I brought the food for a picnic and a blanket for us to sit on. We went to Marvin Park in the Springfield, MO area. We found a nice secluded place and had our lunch. We started kissing and then he got on top of me, just like that couple at the lake. I said, "What are you doing?"

George said, "Don't you like it?"

I said, "No, get off me. I want to go home now."

He said, "Okay."

We got in the car and I took him back to the half-way house, and then I went home.

When I got home I told my Mom what had happened, and she was determined that I never see him again. Plans were made for me to start College early. I was finishing High School on May 5th, and was going to start College on May 6th. I was able to see him two more times before leaving for college. We went on another "picnic" and ended up naked together. I told him I didn't want to get pregnant, so I watched while he masturbated. We were sitting three feet away from each other but he managed to get it all over me. It was hot and sticky and he used my underwear to clean me up. So when I got home I smelled "funky" but I didn't have sex. All this was new to me. I had no idea why his dick got hard or why milky white stuff came out of his dick. I didn't know what to think of it all.

The next time we went for a "picnic" we got naked and we were kissing and before I knew it, George was inside me. I liked it a lot. I thought, "So this is sex."

The next day I went off to college. It was a teacher's college and if I became a teacher and taught for so many years, they would forgive my student loans. I was going to become a teacher. I, who barely said 20 words in a day, was going to talk in front of students. I didn't know how that was going to work.

I liked the classes I was taking. Math and Literature were offered in the summer session. I was on my way to becoming a teacher, I thought. But then George wrote to me. I don't know how he got my address at College. But he was a persuasive character and I was almost 18. I thought by virtue of my age, I would be an adult at 18. Boy, was I stupid. I had no reasoning capabilities at all.

George had joined the Air Force while I was at college and he got assigned to an Air Force Base near Springfield, MO. I quit college and got married. My Mom came to my wedding. My Dad did not. My parents were stuck with the student loan. I didn't feel too bad, with what I went through as a child. I felt free from all that. I was beginning a new life with George.

For our honeymoon we went camping. We had plenty of "picnics"!

It wasn't too long before we conceived Florence. I thought I had the flu; I was throwing up all the time. George took me to the hospital at the Air Force Base. When they told me I was pregnant, I *wasn't* surprised. But I *was* happy. One of the female nurses took me aside and told me I didn't *have* to have the baby. I didn't know what she was talking about. When I later realized that she was talking about an abortion, I was taken aback. Why would I want to have an abortion? It wasn't a moral decision, it was just a common sense decision. Ever since I left my childhood home I was happy for the first time in my life. Being pregnant was a happy event for me.

When I had Florence, my Mom came to see me. My Dad did not.

Soon George was transferred to an Air Force Base in the Mojave Desert of California, 50 miles from Los Angeles. We loved the desert. At first we had a house on the Base. I had a job as the Fire Department secretary and George was a personnel clerk.

George learned to ride motorcycles. He got me a smaller version of his own. I loved riding, but only in the desert. I considered street riding too dangerous. However, when I went over a rail road tie that was buried in the sand, I went flying over the handlebars and had to ride back to the base 20 miles with a broken collar bone. George had diaper duty until I was healed up.

Florence went everywhere with us. We went camping in the desert with other families. We camped under the stars. She slept with us in the middle of our double sleeping bag. It was very cozy.

One day on the base I was walking to the store. All of a sudden I heard this loud BOOM. I and everybody who was out walking had stopped and looked around to see what direction the smoke would come from. Everyone knew that the boom was a plane crash. At the Air Force Base they trained fighter pilots. This pilot did not make it out of the plane before the crash.

There was an investigation to try to determine what was at fault. They had gathered all the pieces of the plane in a large hanger and they asked me to type their notes. They interviewed the wife and asked if they had had a fight recently. They asked her if he had a cold or took any cold medicine the day of the flight. It was hard on the wife, having just lost her husband, but she got through the questioning. I felt sorry for her as I typed the notes.

Later George and I moved off the Base and rented a little two-room house in the foot hills of the desert. I started running every day and got down to 120 pounds. Not too far from the house we found a place that was a hot springs. There were two ways to get to it. We could drive through the desert to Bowen Ranch and park, then hike two miles, of which the last 50 feet was almost directly straight downhill. We nearly crawled down the last five feet. The other way was to drive to Hesperia Dam, park and hike 5 miles. That was my preferred route because it was nearly a flat trail.

Once we reached the hot springs, if we went the short route, we would have to take off all our clothes and ford a waist-high stream that was icy cold from snow melt. If we took the long way, we crossed Deep Creek on a bridge over the canyon. Florence was four years old during this outing. After I got all our clothes to the other side of the stream, George would carry Florence on his shoulders so she wouldn't get cold. Once we were across the stream, there was a 500-foot stretch of beach with warm water that resulted in the mixture of the hot springs water mixing with the cold water of a small waterfall.

Beside the beach and waterfall were three hot springs. One was large and tepid. Another was about the size and heat of a 5-person hot tub. It was perfectly round. And then there was the Crab Cooker, the size and shape of a bathtub. People would bet each other that they couldn't remain submerged more than five seconds. Men simply could not. But women have their reproductive organs on the inside of their bodies, so we could. And the trick of it, I learned, is to slowly slip into the water so that a protective layer of air bubbles surround you. As long as this is the case, you can remain submerged forever. But getting out is a bitch because the minute you disturb this bubble layer, your skin is exposed to the scorching hot water. So you must get out quickly.

My favorite activity at the hot springs was to float on my back in the water beginning at the falls and letting the current sweep me down stream. Then I would swim against the current until I was at the falls again. I would just do that over again until my muscles were nice and exercised. Then I'd lay on the huge rock formation that was warm from volcanic activity deep inside the earth. Clothing was optional.

I recently looked up Deep Creek on YouTube and found that there is now graffiti all over the beautiful rock formations. It's a crying shame. It used to be pristine in the 1970's.

One time we went a different route, driving in the desert to a different foot hill and making our own trail to the hot springs. I guess George didn't want to pay the parking fee at Bowen Ranch. There were all kinds of trails we could follow. We spent all day in the water and sun. It didn't matter what the season was because the water was nice and hot. We dressed for the walk in and out. We shed our clothes once we were there.

When it started to get late, we knew we had to leave before it got dark or we wouldn't find our car. Well, we got lost and it did get dark, and we didn't find our car. Florence was five at the time. When we could no longer walk because we were so tired, George told us to lay down to sleep with Florence between us to keep her warm. We would continue looking for the car in the morning. Well, George must have dreamed how to get to the car because in a few hours, in the dead of the night, we started walking again under a sky full of stars. He soon found where he had left his car. We had to hike up a hill to get to it, but we were soon home.

Another time that we went to the hot springs there must have been a stronger current running off the falls because there appeared a new beach 50 feet across from the large beach and the only way to get to it was by swimming to it. Florence wanted me to take her there. I had been teaching Florence how to swim, but she wasn't a very strong swimmer. When I told her to hold her breath, she would grab the middle of her neck to "hold" her breath.

I told her, "No, holding your breath means not to breathe for a short amount of time." So she quickly learned to swim. To get to this new beach, however, we would have to swim more than 50 feet. She would need me to help her get there.

It was my big idea to have her hold onto my back while I swam us both there. Big mistake. I was a strong swimmer, but her weight dropped us both down to the bottom of the lagoon. When I touched the bottom with my feet, I jumped us both up to catch a breath. But we went back down to the bottom, 12 feet in my estimation. The next time I jumped us more toward the shore of the beach, but only got to gulp some more air and down we went again. This time I was determined to push Florence toward the shore so she could crawl up the beach. I succeeded and watched her crawl while I went down again. Freed from her weight, I was able to swim under water until I got to the shore. I lay there, gulping air until I couldn't move from the spot. I'd many times seen such a scenario in movies, but never before had experienced the exhaustion of a near-drowning.

CHAPTER 6

Should I tell about the time Nina came to visit us in the desert? Maybe not until she dies. Suffice it to say that she made two grown men cry when she left. My husband was heartbroken and sobbed, "I married the wrong sister." I was left with the aftermath of two depressed men. Time would heal the heavy hearted.

I never talked about it to my sister and she doesn't know that I know, but a husband tells his wife everything when they are in a good relationship. I don't blame her and I don't blame him, but it's like a little splinter in my finger that I can't help but worry every now and then, but will never take out.

Living in the desert was a good experience. We had little lizards come in and skitter on the walls. I didn't mind them. But I did mind the Moon Moths. They have huge bodies and wide wingspans. One got into the house and when I swatted it, hundreds of eggs spilled out all over the carpet. Gross!

The moths would often latch onto the screen door where ants would crawl up the other side and grab ahold of them with their mandibles. They couldn't move after that because they were held fast to the screen door by any number of ants who stung them.

We had some hippy dippy neighbors. Floyd and his young wife and baby. Floyd was a drunken old fool. He had a very old truck that would have been a classic if he fixed it up. As it was, it barely ran. Floyd made his living by going up into the mountains and chopping wood for people to use as fire wood.

One night he failed to come down off the mountain. It had snowed all day and he was just stuck up in the mountains. When he finally did make it down the next day, he told us what he had to do to survive. He divided his load of wood into two piles on the ground, lit them on fire and slept between the two. Otherwise, he would surely have frozen to death. All that work gone up in smoke. The next day he loaded up his gas can for the chain saw and went back to work filling up his truck with wood.

Once in a while Floyd would get extra drunk and come home to the wrong house. He would wind up at the back of our house, his truck half-way on our dirt drive, and half-way down the side of the dirt hill. George would get his shovel and try to level out the truck before it went over the side of our hill while Floyd tried driving back onto level ground. Florence and I would be in hysterics watching them.

We didn't have a TV at the time, but this was just as good. We did have a stereo and a record player. I would check out musical masterpieces from the library to play for Florence. I even found some children's stories on records. And children's songs. And of course, I read to Florence all the time. I taught her to read by the time she went to Kindergarten. Her favorite book was Madeline. I read it to her daily.

One day we dropped Florence off at school and it wasn't a school day. We never got the notice that it was a school holiday. Well, it was too far for Florence to walk and I guess we didn't have a phone at that time because soon afterwards, Florence's teacher gave her a ride home. The teacher wanted to make sure that we were at home, so she knocked on the sliding glass door. There were no drapes. We had been sleeping in the living room by the fireplace after partying the night before, and up popped George, hiding his nakedness behind the couch. Up I popped, just to my knees, hiding my nakedness behind the couch. I was trying to tell Jeff to stay down, but up popped Jeff, hiding his nakedness behind the couch.

The teacher wasn't sure if she should leave Florence with us or not. She asked Florence if she was all right with this. Florence said she knew Jeff. He was over quite a bit. And so she let Florence in and said goodbye to three embarrassed goof-balls. We all got dressed and started the day over again. I apologized to Florence but I could tell she was embarrassed for her teacher to see us like that.

Needless to say, we cleaned up our act after that. No more partying all night.

One Fourth of July we decided to go for a drive up into the mountains – George, Florence and me. It was very hot in the desert and we wanted to cool off on top of a particular mountain that George had read about. When we got off the highway and turned left, we were about 20 miles from the bottom of the mountain. I saw that there were dark clouds all around the top of the mountain. I asked George if there was going to be a bad storm. He assured me there was not going to be a storm.

When we got to the top of the mountain it began to snow. It was a real blizzard on the Fourth of July. We quickly found a Forest Ranger Tower and went up the steps to the top of it. There was fierce lightening, so we got down from the tower. We found a neglected shed that was not locked, and we went inside for shelter. There was a mattress on the floor so I put my coat on top of the mattress and put Florence on the coat and George put his coat on top of Florence. Then we both got on either side of her to keep her warm. It was below 32 degrees for it to snow like that, and we were dressed for summer. The coats were in the car just in case. We huddled together for warmth for an hour and then the storm was over. The clouds parted and the three inches of snow quickly melted. We didn't stick around for very long. We already had our adventure and were eager to get back home.

CHAPTER 7

I decided to go into the Air Force Reserves. George had made a career change in the Air Force which meant he would be going to Tech School in Georgia for 9 weeks. He had been working as a personnel clerk and he was so bored. He made the change to be a Load Master on C-5 cargo planes. He had to learn a lot of math to ensure the load would be at the center of gravity for take-off and landing. He got a medal for making 99% overall in his classes. In his job he would also be traveling with the load to supervise the offloading and calculating the weight for the new load they would be taking on, if any. Even if they didn't take on new cargo, he would have to recalculate for any load that was left for another port of call. Sometimes he had to reconfigure the plane into passenger mode. It was very important work and he would be able to travel the world. He was really excited.

I would be going to Basic Training in Georgia for 6 weeks and then to Tech School for 8 weeks. Florence would be sent to my sister, Nina, while we were both gone. Florence would go to school with her two cousins, Bill and Sally.

George decided to take a road trip with Florence before sending her on a plane to Nina. He said he had a great time bonding with Florence. The day before my flight I went to the hot springs by myself early in the morning. I took the long route and enjoyed all the exercise. I knew I was ready for basic training. I had been running 3 miles a day and I was pretty strong.

The first thing we did at Basic Training was to learn to run as a team. They asked who was already a runner and this little petite woman raised her hand. I learned from movies never to volunteer. So it turned out pretty good that they chose the petite woman to be the pace runner because everyone else's legs were longer, and they didn't have to work hard to keep up with her. After running, we did group PT, which was pretty easy for me. I was 24 and in the best shape for me.

When it was time to do the obstacle course, we had been running together for more than three weeks. It was a pretty good obstacle course. I was told to run over a hill where I noticed people standing looking over the hill, afraid to jump. I just ran without measuring the hill and jumped, knowing they wouldn't ask us to do something we couldn't accomplish. It turned out to only be a 10-foot drop. They weren't out to kill us, they only wanted us to obey commands.

There were a couple of water obstacles. One was a rope that you stood on with two ropes at opposite arm's length. The trick of it was not to move the bottom rope too much. And if too many people got on it, everyone made too much movement and everybody fell. I got onto it when no one else was on it and I hurried across before anyone else got on. I was doing well.

The next water obstacle was the hand-over-hand ladder. It was above some really muddy water. My arms were a little flabby, but I had been doing pull-ups in the gym the last few years, so I felt confident I could do this. When a drill instructor saw me, he said, "Oh, this one's gonna fall for sure!" Well, I wasn't about to give him the satisfaction, so even though the rungs were wet from people who had fallen and were made to try again, I set myself to do it. I grabbed the first rung with my right hand, then grabbed it with my left hand. I grabbed the second rung and the third and the fourth, and went really fast until I reached the end.

I was surprised by the stunned drill instructor's face, so I told him, "I didn't want to get my hair wet in that muddy water!"

He laughed and said, "Congratulations! Now keep going."

The only obstacle I could not do, which was more due to self-preservation, was standing on one log and being asked to jump to another horizontal log that was 10-feet away. Well, in my opinion, I knew I couldn't jump horizontally that far, and that if I tried and fell or tried to grip the log, I would come away with a bunch of nasty splinters, and then fall. Fear and self-preservation prevented me from moving without trying to do what I was commanded to do. Finally, the drill instructor said, "Okay, go to the next one." It was the same one who witnessed my small triumph over the water. He understood that I wasn't being a wimp.

When it was all over we all had canned rations, called C-rations. Most of it was edible. Most everyone was soaked and muddy. I was glad I wasn't one of them.

Everything went swimmingly until my husband visited me. I was supposed to be back in the barracks by a certain time. My husband told me it would be alright if I was late.

Well, it wasn't alright. My punishment for being late was that I had to do guard duty every other hour throughout the night for the rest of my stay. That was two weeks of sleep deprivation. But I kept my part of the deal and I told the other girls not to forget to wake me up after their one-hour shift.

On the day of departure, one of the guards on duty fell asleep and I just happened to wake up after my hour of sleep was over. I saw her asleep and told her that if her sleeping on duty had prevented me from getting on the bus on time to get the hell out of there, that I would have ripped her a new one. I was really mad that I was doing my duty every hour and she couldn't even stay awake for one hour.

I didn't believe I was going to get out of there until I was actually on the bus, and then not until we had cleared the gates. I knew it would take a few hours to reach our destination, so I slept with my head against the window. In an hour I woke up, threw out my arms in surprise because I was supposed to be on guard duty again. The guy in the next seat didn't appreciate me grabbing his leg. He swapped his seat with someone else and I went back to sleep.

I was really glad when we were all shown to our individual rooms that we were to stay in for the next week. It was glorious to be alone and to sleep through the night. Tech School was to start the next week and we were to familiarize ourselves with the base in the meantime.

My tech school was X-Ray Specialist. The classes were self-paced. We were given classes in anatomy, electronics, math, physics, and the practical classes in using the X-Ray equipment. The limbs we used were real bones encased in black rubber. We learned how to position for different injuries, how much "juice" to give the machine depending on the width of the limb, and how to develop the film for the resultant x-ray. I did really good in all my classes and was the first to graduate.

A week before I was to leave, the tornado warning sirens went off. We looked out the window and saw that the sky had an ominous green tint to it. The people in charge told us to sit on the floor against the wall and link elbows. There was no basement. So I envisioned us flying through the air with our elbows linked. Some of the girls were crying. I was apprehensive but learned not to anticipate. If the roof blew off I would cry.

Well, the all-clear was given and we were fine. But an area near the base was hit hard. We were taken by bus to the area to direct traffic since they had no power and no traffic signals were working. The devastation we saw was horrific. Houses were reduced to 4-inch long splinters. Whole neighborhoods were flattened. The National Guard was out with us and one of my classmates told me that they were cooking steak, and to go get some. But I was too shy. I just continued to direct traffic.

I was the first to graduate the self-paced classes and was given my ticket home.

CHAPTER 8

After I was flown back to my home in the desert I went back to work for the Air Force Fire Department at the Base. Most of the firefighters were young, great-looking guys. But I have to admit that I was attracted to an older man who was in his 30's. He knew I had a crush on him and whenever he had Tower duty, he would invite me up to learn something new. The Fire Department Tower overlooked the runways. It was also the radio dispatch center. To get to it, there were two flights of stairs and then a ladder up the wall to a square hatch that opened upwards.

The fire department had been planning night operations in coordination with the Flight Tower personnel and the F-4 fighter jet pilots. It was a test of compliance with Standard Operating Procedures (SOPs) in the case of a pilot making an emergency landing. In preparation, the cable that the pilots hooked during an emergency landing was inspected and found to be in good condition. The firemen then rewound the cable, making sure it didn't tangle on its way back inside its holdings. Radio checks were made in the pumper trucks, the ladder trucks and the Chief and Deputy Chief.

When the day was done I asked the Chief if I could observe the exercise up in the tower. Permission was granted, and as it got dark, I made my way up the ladder to the trap door of the tower. It wouldn't budge. I knocked on the square door and heard a chair being dragged off the door. That's what the firemen do when they are using the urinal and don't want to be disturbed.

When the door was opened, my nose confirmed my thoughts. The cool air from downstairs coming through the trap door quickly dissipated the odor. When I was completely through the door, Jonsey shut the door and replaced the chair back on the top of the door. It was almost completely dark now, and the exercise would soon begin.

The fire department tower and the flight tower were about 500 feet away from each other. I could barely see figures in the fading light. Both towers went dark and instrument panels lit up. We were into it now. Jonsey turned to his dispatching duties while I watched him work the instrument panels.

Outside the F-4 pilots were climbing into their jets and strapping in. One at a time they sped down the runway into the westerly winds that typically blew after sunset. Both jets in the air now using their afterburner to gain altitude fast. It was very noisy this close to the runway.

As planned, the first jet declared an emergency to the flight tower and the flight tower relayed the emergency situation to the fire department dispatcher. Jonsey dispatched pumper 1 and 2 to standby for a cable landing. The pilot of the first jet caught the cable with his tail hook and came to a screeching halt seconds later. Pumper 1 dispatched two firefighters to get the "unconscious" fighter pilot out of his cockpit. Then pumper 1 dispensed foam flame retardant all over the jet. The firemen were sure to close the cockpit first. No need to make a mess out of their instruments inside the jet.

Meanwhile the second jet declares an emergency landing with a non-operating tail hook. He will be landing on the north-south runway. The flight tower and the fire department tower coordinate to put up the barrier, made of heavy nylon webbing that is automatically raised over the end of the runway to arrest the speed of the jet in a safe manner.

Pumper 1 and 2 are dispatched to the north-south runway and wait for the second emergency landing. The pilot makes a messy landing within the webbed barrier, is rescued and then foam is pumped onto the jet.

It was all very exciting to be a part of.

When it was all over, the pumpers had to switch to water to clean up the foam from the jets and the runway, and supervise replacing the cable and barrier system back in their receptacles.

Jonsey knew this would take a while, so he turned toward me and gave me a great big hug, saying, "Wasn't that great?"

"It sure was," I said

Jonsey gave me a kiss which I enjoyed and returned. He carried me to the waist-high counter and laid me down while he slipped my panties off.

I said, "What about the flight tower?"

"They are too far away," he said.

We had to hurry, finishing before the foam was disbursed from the runway. But we had fun.

When we were finished, Jonsey got a radio call from the flight tower. They said, "Give your girlfriend the night-vision goggles and point her in our direction."

He gave me the binoculars and I saw three grinning airmen holding a big sign that said "10" and one of them had his own goggles looking back at me.

I looked back at Jonsey and showed my disapproval, but then I laughed and said, "Jonsey, you're a fool." And I left through the little trap door and went home.

CHAPTER 9

George was still at Tech School and would be for another four weeks. Florence flew back home from Nina's house and we were just settling back into our lives when a fierce lightning storm came our way. There was no rain, just ferocious winds making our roof rattle. The wind howled like a live animal. We hunkered down listening to the thunder. One crack of thunder was so loud that I ventured to look out the window. A fire had started in the next valley to the east and was coming our way, fast. I got Florence in the car and stopped by our neighbor's house and got her and her baby in my car. I drove us to the Air Force Base to a friend's house. She agreed to let us stay the night.

The next morning I went to the Fire Department to work and asked them if they would check out my house, to see if it was still standing. I asked them to go inside and check out the condition.

When they came back, they said, "Your neighbor's house is gone, except for the chimney. There are dead rabbits everywhere, but your house still stands. Your clothes smell like smoke, but nothing else is ruined."

Our house had a 50-foot clearing all around it. That's what saved it. If I hadn't picked up the neighbor and her baby, they would have surely died in the fire.

When I returned home the area looked like a moon scape. Gone were the many waist-high creosote bushes, which had covered the rabbit holes. Beside every rabbit hole was a dead rabbit. It was a pitiful sight.

We stayed there another week before I decided to leave. Florence and I got a ride from the base's Fire Station Chief to the bus station in town, and we rode the bus to Anna's house, which was just outside Springfield, MO. It took us two days and two nights. The lady in the third seat of our row snored so loudly that Florence and I had to be strong not to laugh every time she "honked".

My sister, Anna, lived about 10 miles from our childhood home on the outskirts of Springfield, MO. Anna offered to let us live with her. Her son, John, was barely one year older than Florence, and he had an upper bunk he wasn't using. I could sleep on the couch. It was cozy, and it worked out great. When I showed Anna how swollen my ankles were from sitting on the bus for two days, she got out her foot massager, filled it with water, and I soaked my feet and ankles for hours. It was about three days before they went back to normal.

I got a job right away because I typed 99 words a minute on their typing test with only one mistake. I got hired as a word processor at Bryant & Bryant, an accounting firm. I worked for their tax department. They didn't have a desk for me yet, so they used me as a messenger at first. The first thing they asked me to messenger was a tax return for the Mayor. They told me to take a cab and ask to be taken to City Hall. Well, I had never taken a cab before, but I knew the bus system, and that it would take me to City Hall. I got on the bus, and about mid-way to my stop, the bus stopped suddenly. The large envelope slid off my lap and disappeared between my seat and the wall of the bus. I was sitting in the back of the bus. I looked to see if it was on the ground under my seat, but, no. It was permanently embedded inside the end-console that made up the back wall of the bus. The lady sitting across the aisle from me saw it happen. She looked at me with pity in her eyes, but she didn't want to get involved. She said nothing, and just got out at her stop.

I told the bus driver what happened and asked him if I could get a maintenance man to remove the console cover so I could retrieve the folder. He looked at me like I was a Martian.

He said, "Well, lady, that envelope is going to stay in that console beside your seat until the day this bus is retired and sold for scrap."

I couldn't believe it. I would have to go back to the secretary of vice president of the tax department and tell her what happened. I would probably lose my job. When I got back and told the secretary, she said, "You'd better tell that to the vice president of the tax department, and let him decide what to do."

I related the entire story to the vice president of the tax department and he completely lost it. He was laughing so hard that he was crying. He said, "That's the best 'first-day' story I've ever heard. We better hurry up and get you a desk so you can start doing what we hired you for."

I said, "But what about the Mayor's tax return?"

He said, "It will probably never see the light of day before the statute of limitations is over. In the meanwhile, we can just print the damn thing out again, and call a messenger service to deliver it."

I said, "I'm not fired?"

He said, "No. It was an unexpected accident, and there's apparently nothing we can do about it."

The very next day they got my desk and word processing equipment installed.

Bryant & Bryant was going through a high-growth period and they soon merged with a London firm, creating Bryant & Cove ("B&C"). All the letterhead, envelopes and everyone's business cards had to be reordered. The word processing department had a lot of extra work to do in the merger. All the documents that were used daily for clients had to now contain the firm's name change.

The way they decided to do it, was to pay a computer consultant to scan in each document into a Lanier word processing document, and we would go through each document for scanning errors. This was 1978, so scanners were not what they are today. There were many scanning errors, and there were many documents. So B&C asked if I would supervise a night shift with one helper that they would hire to make these documents usable. The firm had generous night-work benefits. If you worked four hours past 4 p.m., you got a dinner allowance, even if you didn't go out for dinner. Then if you worked past 10 p.m., you got a transportation allowance, even if your car was in their garage. I was working from 1 p.m. to 9 p.m., but many times I would work until midnight. I was tireless back then, when I was 28. It took six weeks, but we got them all done.

I was given a nice raise, along with all the overtime and night-work benefits. My bank account was growing. At Anna's house, we split the bills, except for her mortgage. I went grocery shopping at the commissary at the nearby Army base since I was a Reservist. That saved us a lot of money.

And then George called me out of the blue. He was done with his technical training and was working at an Air Force Base, in California, as a Load Master for the C-5 cargo planes. He loved the job and he loved me. The one thing he said that made sense to me was "I'll be gone a lot, so you won't have to put up with me as much."

I said, "Okay."

CHAPTER 10

Florence and I packed up and took a plane to Sacramento, where George picked us up and drove us to Vacaville, nearby the Air Force Base. Florence would be going into the second grade, and we found an apartment across the street from the elementary school. I soon found a job at the local newspaper. I operated one of their two automated typesetters used for advertisement. A lady who had been there many years trained me, and I picked it up quickly. I worked there for close to a year.

One day the editor asked me into his office. I had worked on an advertisement for a funeral parlor who had been a long-time client. He handed me the ad that I had worked on, and I was aghast to see that I had re-written their logo as "Let us scatter your asses!" It should have been "Let us scatter your ashes!"

I asked, "Am I fired?"

He answered, "No, but you must be more careful."

From then, I was asked to learn some of the other automated typesetting machines. One was a dedicated headline maker. Another was used for news articles, the mainstay of the paper. I was being very useful. I was pretty happy.

I had been watching the newspaper want ads, especially the Sacramento Bee for other word processing jobs. I just happened to see that the Sacramento office of Bryant & Cove needed a word processor. I applied right away, and drove up to Sacramento to interview. The Managing Partner, Mr. Grainly, interviewed me. Then he walked up to the floor-to-ceiling windows and wanted to show me the view. It was a nice view. Then I felt him put his hand around my waist. I said, "Yes, it's a nice view." I was nice and trim, having run 3 miles a day since Basic Training. I didn't mind if he wanted to touch me. He led me to the door and opened it, saying, "We'll let you know."

I started to walk out, but his secretary said, "This check is for your travel."

I said, "Thanks. That's really nice." It was a 30-mile drive.

The next day I got the job. I asked George if we could move to Sacramento so I wouldn't have so long of a commute. He agreed, since I had to drive to work every week-day and he only had to drive to the base once every three weeks, and was home for about a week between trips. We found an apartment complex that had a gated community. It had a swimming pool and a hot tub.

I would drive Florence to her school right before heading off to work. She was in third grade now.

It was now 1980, when B&C decided to get a computer – one for the whole office. It was an Apple IId. They let me be the computer operator, and I learned it very quickly. The staff was asked to try learning the computer either before or after work. Someone would come in at 6 a.m. just to find that I was already on it. I read the manual and learned the document filing system. There wasn't much to it. It only had a 1 MB storage capacity.

As time went by, the firm saw the need for a PC on every desk. Whenever they got a new program installed on the computers, they would first ask me to take a look at it and see if I could learn it. One of the programs was rBase. It was a database program. I played around with it and read the manual and pretty soon I had input all our clients' due dates for tax returns, financial statements, and any other deadline.

I was able to create reports from scratch, before there were end-user menus. The manual told how. Then when I went on a vacation to Florida, the firm called me asking me to tell someone how to run the reports. So I ran through the procedures, step by step, until they were able to print out all the reports they needed.

When I came back from my vacation the firm asked me to set up a menu system so that anyone could do the data entry, run the reports, etc. So I read the manual and taught myself how to create end-user menus and help screens. This was well before Microsoft Word.

For word processing we used Word Star, then as the years went on, we used a series of different, ever more sophisticated word processing software and equipment. We used Word Perfect before it was perfect, then the firm settled on a proprietary dedicated word processing system called Lanier. Then we switched to the all-purpose PC and used Microsoft Word, Excel, Power Point, and a database program called dBase. I learned dBase just like I had learned rBase beforehand. The only difference was that dBase did have built in menus. I read the manual and set up the client database. I was able to import all the clients' due dates into dBase, and built in custom data-entry screens and help screens. DBase was much more sophisticated that rBase. It was very simple to set up reports. I trained the other secretaries to use the program.

Not too long after we were all using Microsoft programs, I heard that Bill Gates was going to be in town speaking about his programs. It was so interesting how he demonstrated Excel, doing increasingly more sophisticated tasks. He then showed how to use all Microsoft programs in an integral way, linking Excel spreadsheets together and creating a graph, importing it into a letter in Word. He showed that his Microsoft Office set of programs was all you would ever need to run a business.

The only problem I had with his programs, was that every program had to be licensed for one computer only. So if you had 500 computers, you would need to buy 500 Microsoft sets of programs. After his talk, there was an open microphone for questions. I got in the line and asked when he was going to allow for site licenses. He knew exactly what I meant – one license for one business site. So, if a business had multiple offices, each office would have to buy their own site license. But that was much preferable to having to buy a program for each computer.

Bill Gates kind of laughed and said, "I don't think that will occur very soon." Yeah, he was raking in the money hand over fist, and the audience knew it, because they kind of gave a collective laugh at such a notion as a site license. Of course, now, site licenses are common place. Even free updates are readily available every time you turn off your computer. You have the choice to either shut down, or restart and update.

When you first buy a new computer, these updates take a long time, and so Best Buy and other similar companies, like Office Depot, offer for a fee, to do all the program installations and upgrades when you buy a new computer.

Bryant & Cove had another growth spurt in 1989 when they merged with Janell White. They had become Bryant & White ("B&W"). Again, they had to order all new letterhead, envelopes and everyone's business cards.

The Word Processing departments of both firms merged. Janell White was using Macintoch's and Bryant & Cove was using PC's. It was decided that we would convert all PC documents to Macintosh format. I told them that I was in charge of that function in the previous merger. So their IT department found a software that would automatically convert MS Word to Macintosh Word. They showed me how to run it, and at night I would transform the documents, diskette by diskette from MS Word to Macintosh Word. It only took 3 weeks. And there were no scanner errors to deal with.

I worked with B&W for 13 years. During that time my marriage was falling apart due to George's drug usage. He started with marijuana, but he soon graduated to Cocaine. He was doing Cocaine one day when he asked me if I wanted to try it. He said it was great for sex. I think that was the first time I ever stood up for myself and I said, "What, are you crazy?"

In the meantime Florence was 9 when I decided I'd like to have another child. Florence was really smart and she did so well in all her classes. She still played with Barbie dolls and "taught" them how to read. My biological clock was ticking as I was almost 30. George didn't take much convincing. Florence had been born in 1972, and her new sister, Karen, was born in 1982, almost exactly ten years apart. Florence loved Karen from the time I brought her home from the hospital. As soon as

Florence got home from school, she would look in on Karen and if she was playing, Florence would play with her.

I went back to work when Karen was 9 weeks old. We found a nice babysitter that wasn't too far away. Florence also went to the babysitter after school. That's when I decided I wanted to go back to college. I worked full time during the day while I went to a private university full time at night. I finished in four years and got my Bachelor of Business Administration, with an emphasis in Management of Information Systems. I got a very basic understand of how computers worked and how to program in Cobalt. But computers were changing every year.

One thing I was very proud of is the math classes I took. I started at Pre-Algebra, and finally understood the concepts, that an equation has to balance, so if you add or subtract something on one end of the equation, you have to add or subtract the same amount to the other side of the equation. That's how you isolate the variable to find out its value. For example, given the equation 6+x=10. First you have to isolate the x by subtracting the 6 from the left side of the equation and also subtracting 6 from the right side of the equation, getting (6-6)+x=10-6. So, 0+x=4, or x=4. Then you can proof it by plugging 4 into the original equation in place of the x. 6+4=10.

Then I went on to Algebra 1, 2 and 3. Then Trigonometry, Logic, Calculus 1, 2 and 3. I got A's in everything except went down to a B for Calculus 2 and a C for Calculus 3.

I was glad when all the math was over. Then I took Earth Sciences and computer programming. I did a paper on AT&T for my final class, how the government decided it was a monopoly, and forced it to divest itself of Bell Laboratories. AT&T then concentrated on long-distance and the newly formed Bell Telephone concentrated on local phone calls. During the beginning of the break-up, AT&T workers sat on one side of the building, and AT&T workers sat on the other side. Colored duct tape outlined each entity, and each was told not to talk to the others. They were now competitors.

Shortly after the break-up of AT&T, many other long-distance phone companies sprouted up. Then came the cell phones and cell towers that all but eliminated the need for long-distance phone companies.

CHAPTER 11

When Florence became a teen-ager she would no longer do as I said. She would go out with boys much older than her. At 15 she became pregnant. I didn't know it at the time, but the man she brought home, Greg, wasn't the father of her child. They both knew it, but they wanted to be a couple, and I wanted Florence to remain at home.

Karen was five at the time, and would walk home from school and be minded by Florence and Greg.

I always loved to sleep in on Saturday so I was constantly telling Karen and Florence not to wake me in the morning. Well, at 6 a.m. one Saturday Florence knocks on my door and I simply yelled out the door, "Didn't I tell you not to wake me up so early!"

Florence said, "I'm in labor."

I said, "Oh! How long?"

She said, "Since 4 a.m."

I said, "Pack a bag. I'll take you to the hospital right now."

She said, "Shouldn't we wait?"

I told her, "I had you in 20 minutes after the ambulance took me to the hospital. And the first baby is usually the fastest."

So we got to the hospital and Florence was given an epidural. Then occasionally we would hear a scream from another room. "What is that?" Florence asked. Nobody knew what to tell her. I didn't want to scare her. They took her right into the birthing room and she pushed just a couple of times when the baby's head came to be under the part of the pelvis bones that temporarily separate to let the head out. It was bone against baby head bone and Florence screamed once. When it was all over Florence said, "Is that all there is to it?" She was happy as a clam. She named her baby Anne.

Florence had a chance to go to an alternative school where girls could take their babies to school where they had a day care. Florence went for about a year, but then quit school because she wanted to get a job. Later, she tested for her GED and received it.

She had a series of jobs, mostly minimum wage jobs. Greg would watch baby Anne all day and Karen after school. We were a three-generation household and for a while it was good. We played Monopoly together and we had fun.

I liked riding my bike on a 27-mile bike trail from Sacramento to Folsom Dam. At first it was pretty hard for me because it was a series of up-hills until the Dam was reached. At times I would have to walk up some of the hills until I was fit enough to ride standing up. Most times I turned back before reaching the Dam. But I remember the first time I reached the Dam. I was so proud of myself for finally making it. There was a little store at the Dam where I bought some food and something to drink.

When I was fully refreshed, I got back on my bike and was thinking how easy it was going to be coming home because it was basically all downhill. I was in for a big surprise. The very first hill I picked up some speed and was horrified when I saw the hair-pin turn in the trail. The trail was only six feet wide and at the far edge at the hair-pin turn was a sheer cliff. I couldn't stop in time, so I took the turn at an extreme lean with the edge of my tires barely skimming the far edge of the trail. I was leaning at nearly a 30 degree angle. I didn't fall, but I was shaking with adrenaline afterwards.

The rest of the ride home was uneventful, but fun. The trip to the Dam took three hours, but the trip home took 45 minutes. It was my favorite thing to do on the weekends. And I continued running three miles a day most week-day mornings. It really helped with stress, especially during the tax season at work.

When George came home from a particular trip, he told me that they had been to Granada, where Argentinian soldiers were holding U.S. medical students hostage. The news had been reporting on it in a general informational way because the US government was not letting anything leak. So I made a mistake by telling my co-worker that George had been to Granada and was dodging bullets while hurrying medical students into the back of the C-5 cargo plane. While I was out of the office for lunch, George had called and my co-worker asked him if what I had said was true. He adamantly denied it and when I returned his call he sternly told me never to talk about his work to anyone ever again. He said the trip to Granada was top secret. Well, why did he tell me about it? When I got off the phone my co-worker said, "Well was he in Granada or not?" In a flat voice I told her, "He was never there." I don't know whether she believed me or not. It didn't matter to me.

One tax season the tax professionals I worked for needed a special project to be done on the computer with the database I had designed. They were on a real time crunch. We worked well into the early morning hours. When I got back home, it was 3 a.m. where I found George and his father sitting on the couch. My father-in-law said to me, "How long has this been going on?" I told him I was working on a project. He didn't believe me, but I knew George did.

George would know if I was having an affair. He always told me about his flings. He had a lady in Colorado that he saw for a week every year. I guess he really liked that movie we saw, "Same Time Next Year," where a couple did the same thing. One day he told me that his lady friend from Colorado was in town with her three kids. I didn't ask if any of those kids were his. But he actually expected me to let them spend the night in our apartment. That was the second time I stood up for myself.

I said, "You put them up in a hotel room. I don't even want to meet your girlfriend." The nerve!

CHAPTER 12

George was heavily involved in drugs. I was very concerned about him losing his job and told him, "Look what you risk losing – half your pay for life, free healthcare for both of us, and our kids until they are 18. You are only six months away from retiring with 20 years. Don't you want to retire?"

"You don't know what you're talking about," he said. "They only test those that are under my rank." He was a Staff Sergeant.

One day I heard him on the phone making arrangements to bring someone some drugs.

I said, "So now you're a dealer?"

He repeated, "You don't know what you're talking about."

I said, "Do you think your commander will understand? If you leave the house tonight, I'm going to call your commander and tell him what you've been up to."

He didn't leave that night at all.

Later that week, George went off on one of his Load Master jobs, traveling with the cargo that he balances with precision. The next day he was home again. It really surprised me because I was so used to him being gone for ten days at a time, then home for a week. I asked him what happened. He said the flight was cancelled.

The next day he went to the base dressed in his blues, which is his dress uniform. He usually dresses in a green flight suit. Then he came home about the time I did from work. This occurred regularly for the next two weeks.

"What's going on?" I asked.

He said, "I'm being the proctor for testing students."

I bought it. But in reality he needed a good proctologist! He finally told me what was going on when he was about to be put in the brig, because he was about to be gone for a lengthy period of time and there was going to be a court martial.

The truth turned out that he had loaded the cargo of his most recent flight, and in the middle of the flight he discovered that he had miscalculated the position of the load. His judgment had been affected by his daily use of marijuana. He would actually toke up heavily before he drove to the base 30 miles away.

All might have been perfectly fine if he had just told the pilot that he made a mistake and that they might want to land for a re-calculation of the load. But no! He decided to move the entire load in mid-flight.

As he shoved the huge load forward a whole foot, the aircraft became nose-heavy and the pilots had to do some fancy flying to prevent a nose-dive of their C-5 cargo plane.

The pilot yelled, "What the hell are you doing back there?"

George finally told them what had happened. The pilot radioed the nearest base for clearance for an emergency landing, and to have the MPs meet the aircraft.

George was escorted to the hospital where a urine sample was demanded. He said he couldn't go at the moment and needed to drink some water. He consumed large quantities of water, thinking he could dilute his urine and beat the drug test. Well, that never works. The only thing that works is not taking drugs for a month or more. I thought he was smart enough to know that.

I was involved in his Court Marshal; I testified against him.

He spent a few more weeks in the brig before they dishonorably discharged him. I moved with Karen into a two-bedroom apartment across town. Florence and Greg were already living away from home in their own apartment. When George got out of the brig, he had no idea where I had gone. That's the way I wanted it.

But he tracked me down somehow. I needed a different plan. I asked my Mom, who had retired to Texas, if I could move in with her until I got back on my feet. I left a job that I had been at for 13 years to move all the way from California to Texas. That way I was sure to get rid of George. We had been married 20 years at that point. I didn't want to get a divorce because I wanted never to get married again. I wanted there to be an obstacle to any hasty marriage. And so I didn't get a divorce for 20 years after that.

Anna and Mom were living together in Texas. There were three bedrooms, so Karen and I took up residence in one of them.

In Texas I found a job right away. I took a general test that had a lot of math in it. Lucky for me. I was confident that I had done well on the test. The supervisor told me they definitely wanted to hire me, but the salary would be low because I hadn't done well on the test. So I accepted the job on their terms. It was a law firm that did personal injury litigation.

I stayed there for several months at that low pay and then called in one day that I was quitting. The supervisor said, "But you did so well on the test." So I caught her in a lie. That was another reason I didn't want to continue working there.

I then got a job as a secretary for the department of Quality Assurance and Utilization at a local hospital. I worked there for a little over a year. But even they paid much less than I was used to.

CHAPTER 13

When Karen was 12, I decided to research the different areas of the US to see where the highest-growing economy at the time was. I left Karen with my Mom and Anna until I got a job so I could bring her to wherever home was going to be. I had job interviews lined up in St. Louis, Louisville, and Des Moines. The Midwest was not only growing its economy, but the cost of living was much lower than on either coast.

When I drove into St. Louis, it looked so trashy, so I just kept going toward Louisville. I interviewed at a job at a local hospital in the department of home health. They said they would let me know in a couple of weeks. So in the meanwhile I interviewed at every nearby hospital in and around Louisville. I got the job at the first hospital I interviewed with as a secretary to the Home Health Director. When I got back to a room I was renting, there were a lot of calls from the other hospitals wanting me to work for them. So I found out I was still highly marketable.

I saved up for a few months and then called my Mom to get Karen ready for a flight I had arranged to bring her to Louisville. I had moved to a three-bedroom rental house when Karen joined me. I enrolled her in the local middle school and thought everything would be fine.

The first day that Karen walked home from school, she was mugged by two kids. They actually kicked her in the head while she was saying,

"Why are you doing this?" When she got home and called me at work to tell me about it, I told my boss I had an emergency and would be back as soon as possible. I drove home and picked Karen up and drove her to my work. She said her head hurt, and I said, "I'm sorry honey. I'm going to pick you up from school from now on."

For the next week or so I brought her to my work after school. My boss told me I couldn't do it anymore. So I continued to pick her up at 3 from school and drove her home before returning to work. I used my lunch hour for this purpose. The boss was happier with that.

When Karen turned 13 it was like a switch turned on in her personality. She started hanging out with the wrong type of people and started doing drugs. It was like she was following in Florence's footsteps. When Karen was 14 I talked to Florence to see if she could stay with her because Florence was a stay-at-home mom. She had three young kids of her own, and I thought she would be a good influence on Karen.

Karen stayed with Florence for several months, but Florence finally told me that she had had enough. I sent Florence the money for a plane trip, and the next week I picked Karen up at the airport. I was shocked by how Karen looked. She was dressed to kill. She was wearing a low-cut mini-dress with laced up tall black velvet boots. While waiting for her luggage, she was sucking on her finger, so she was giving the all-out "look at me, I'm sexy but I'm still a little girl" message and people were staring at her.

One day her school called me to say she was a no-show at school. I took off from work and went home to find she was asleep in her bed. I woke her up and told her to get dressed for school. I drove her to school and sat next to her in every class. I even gave a little report in front of the class because I knew something about the subject. Karen was so embarrassed.

After middle school I enrolled her in Lincoln Prep School because I knew she was smart. But she couldn't keep up with the work because she was still taking drugs. When a person is doing drugs, the most important thing on their mind is where to get more drugs. School work isn't even on their radar screen. She had met a guy named Jerry who was the same age and in the same predicament, and they both moved into his father's house. Karen became pregnant at 15 and at 16 she had Jane. Karen and Jerry both quit school and took the GED. They both passed. They were both smart, but they were just stupid with life decisions.

Meanwhile, I was working two jobs, a full-time job and a part-time job. I didn't have to be at work until 2 p.m. for a word processing job I had found at a large firm, and so I worked part time in the morning being a file clerk at a hospital. I got a lot done in the mornings and cleared up their back-log in no time. Then I was asked to take inventory of their dead-storage files in the back room. I was about half-way done when my night job started to offer overtime for a long-term project. I took advantage of the higher pay and told my part-time job that I was giving them a one-week notice. I showed them what I had done in their dead-storage room, and they were impressed that I had gotten so far. It was a menial but meaningful job. However, I could make so much more money at my other job doing overtime.

Once in a while I would be asked to babysit Jane and I would be glad to do it, but I wasn't the type of person to clamor for time with my grandkids. I hadn't seen Florence's kids for 15 years. We were half-way across the country from them. They grew up knowing George, but I only came for a visit once when Cary was 3, Tina was 5 and Gail was 6. Florence was still living with her drug-addict boyfriend and I didn't want much to do with that situation.

I had just gotten a new car and Karen asked me if she and her boyfriend could borrow it to go to a concert because their car was unreliable. I agreed as long as they were back by the time I had to go to work the next day. I waited and waited for them to get back. It was nearly time for me to leave for work. They didn't call me or anything. This was before cell phones were affordable by everyone. When they finally did show up, they told me that it had been very muddy at the outdoor concert and everyone was sliding down the hill, including them. Oh, and by the way, we gave some people rides home. So I was envisioning the inside of my new car being a virtual pig-sty. They said, "Oh, but we cleaned it up good as new, except for a little mud on the inside of the roof." I didn't want to ask what how that happened. I decided that was the end of my lending my car to them. Once and over.

CHAPTER 14

Jerry and Karen were tired of living with Jerry's father because he had them working fast-food jobs and making them give the money to him. They wanted to move out and get a place of their own. The only thing was, they were still under 18. They couldn't get an apartment. The best they could do was get a room in a house. They did pretty well by getting the upper floor of a house that had all the accoutrements of an apartment. And I didn't even have to co-sign for them. The guy had pity on them and he agreed to let them rent his upstairs.

When they reached 18, they moved into an apartment in just outside of Louisville. It wasn't long before Karen and Jerry got involved with Methamphetamines. Karen decided she liked the meth dealer better than Jerry, so she moved in with him. She was so hooked on Meth that she had little capacity for good judgment. Jerry became Jane's primary care-giver. He would hardly let Karen see her. One day when I picked up Karen for an rare outing, she asked, "What happens if you have bruises on your kidneys?"

I said, "What do you mean?"

She showed me these humungous bruises on her skin just at the kidney level on both sides of her back. I asked her who did that to her, Jerry or the drug dealer? She wouldn't tell me. It could have been either one. I hated them both. I was going to do something criminal if I knew who to do it to. I let it go but I never forgot it. I told her to go to the hospital if she pees blood. That's all I could do. She was being controlled by meth and whoever beat her.

Worse news was just around the corner. It so happened that when Karen and Jerry were living together that one of them, or both of them, were looking at child pornography on their computer. It turned out to be a sting operation orchestrated by Governor of Kentucky. FBI agents busted their door down in the early hours of the morning and confiscated their computer. At first they arrested Jerry because they assumed he would have been the one to do something so despicable. But Jerry stuck to his story that it was Karen who was looking at the pictures. Since the computer was accessible by both parties, it was difficult for them to know for sure. Karen confided in me that it was really Jerry, but he was raising Jane; and Jerry convinced her that it was better for Jane if Karen was the one to be blamed. I told her not to do this. Don't take the blame for Jerry. I told her we could raise Jane together.

She was arrested on the doorstep of my apartment. The FBI had finished their investigation and somehow decided it was Karen. They told her that she had 5 counts against her, and each count carried a 5-year sentence. They told her if she took a plea bargain, she would bring that down to one count with a 5-year sentence. She finally agreed to the plea bargain.

Karen told me her sentencing was on a certain date and would I come to it so she could see me before they ship her off to prison. I agreed.

I was the only one in the audience of the court room. She had asked others to come, but nobody else did.

We were able to have a short conversation before the case began. She wore an orange jump suit and had her feet shackled with a chain that came up to her hands and then around her waist. It was a pitiful site to see a 19-year old girl like that, let alone my own flesh and blood.

The judge sentenced her to three years in prison and two years of supervised probation. One condition was that she could not have access to the internet until after her probationary term was over. And, finally, she was to have no contact with any children. That's when Karen broke down crying. She asked her lawyer to ask the judge if she could have contact with her own daughter. The judge had already gone into her chambers, so I was wondering if she would come out again. She did, and she said that she could have contact with her own daughter.

Karen and I corresponded while she was in a federal prison in Florida. She told me how she was in a cell with two other women. There was one set of bunk beds and an inflatable mattress on the floor. She, being the newbie, was assigned to the mattress on the floor.

She said there was a certain etiquette that they followed. Since the "dining area" and the toilet were in such close proximity, the one on the toilet would say to the one who was eating, "I'm sorry to be shitting in your kitchen." And the other would say, "I'm sorry to be eating in your bathroom."

Karen and the two others were given a monthly supply of maxi-pads that stuck to their panties. But Karen found after a few months, that she didn't need them anymore. She was pregnant with the drug dealer's child. Since they had a stock-pile of maxi-pads, they would sometimes stick them to the bottom of their shoes to wipe up a big spill on the floor. They were more absorbent than Bounty.

Karen worked with the prison's social worker to find a couple to adopt her child. There were proposals that Karen was allowed to look through and she chose a couple in San Diego.

The prison social worker made sure Karen was given more protein, milk and fruit so the baby didn't suffer. She also got the lower bunk. When it came time for Karen to deliver, the guards took her to the local hospital and expected her to give birth while still wearing her shackles and chains. The nurses and doctor refused to participate unless the chains were removed. For a while there was a stand-off. Finally, the guards removed the chains and shackles, but handcuffed her hand to the bed. A nurse said, "Believe me, she is not going to do any running after giving birth."

The baby turned out to be a boy and Karen refused to look at him or to hold him. The San Diego couple was there and they received their baby. I always wonder whether the baby inherited any terrible traits from either parent. I think maybe it was a good thing that Karen was in prison for the term of her pregnancy. She had no contact with Meth and she went through a rehabilitation program. After the three years of prison Karen had to be drug-tested every month for two years. And every year on her birthday she had to be photographed for the Sex Offender Registry.

Because of the federally-funded rehab program, Karen was eligible for school grants. So she took classes and was even allowed to use the computer for research and to submit her papers to the professor. The only condition was that both Karen and I would allow an inspection of each of our hard drives at any time for the two year probationary period. We both agreed.

After all was said and done, Karen told me that if she had known how horrible the ordeal would be that she would have never taken the rap for Jerry. Now, every time she wanted to see Jane, she would have to explain to Jerry's many girlfriends, who always seemed to have a new baby, that she would not be allowed to be alone with her baby.

Jerry was a real son of a bitch. He would purposefully get his girlfriends pregnant and then throw them out. He even did this to the daughter of the drug dealer. Pay-back, no doubt.

Jerry moved to Georgia for a job and took Jane with him. We didn't know how bad that was for Jane until both Jerry and his then-girlfriend were both taken to jail for domestic violence, leaving Jane alone in the home. Jane is very smart. She took the opportunity to call the Child Protective Services of Georgia and told them she had been the victim of abuse by her father for years. She also relayed that she was left alone while both adults were arrested.

The Child Protective agency came to get Jane right away. They placed her with a family who has a daughter that Jane knew from school. Jane had them call me and plans were made to fly Jane back to Kentucky on the premise of visiting her grandmother. When she arrived I made arrangements for Karen to see a Kentucky family law attorney for her to get sole custody of Jane.

Jerry was prohibited from contacting his victim in any way. When I looked up his Face Book page he had posted pictures of Jane handling hand guns and machine guns in the desert. There were also open beer containers near the fire arms. I printed out those pictures for the lawyer.

Then I looked at Jane's Face Book page and there was a message from her dad saying, "I will hunt you down." I printed that out and gave it to the lawyer.

Karen got custody of Jane, no problem. Karen has been home-schooling Jane and I have been paying for computerized classes for $175 per month. It's worth it to me that Jane gets a good education and that she is not exposed to bad influences from school mates the way that Karen was.

CHAPTER 15

I was looking in the personals one day and came across an inmate who said, "I've got a story. Want to read it?" Being a voracious reader and having lived alone for 15 years, the ad kind of peaked my interest. And the inmate's picture was very handsome.

I wrote to the inmate, whose name was Tom Baker, and who was Danish. At one time he was a member of the Danish Parliament of the progressive party. He was a very interesting fellow. He did have a story, in fact he had two. The first book was called *Operation White Terror*. The second book was called *The Maracaibo Plot*. He had typed them each up on a manual typewriter and wanted me to type them into the computer. I told him I could scan them in and then watch out for scanning errors. He told me he would split the royalties with me 60/40. If I had known then what kind of work this would entail, I would never have contacted him in the first place.

For one thing, the scanning did not go well because he would put pen-mark corrections on the copy to be scanned. Other pages were copied and the copy had cut off the ends of some pages.

The first book took a little more than two years to scan, fix, edit, have him proof, and then have him send corrections to me. When he finally said it was ready to send to a publisher, I researched and chose

Wayne Publishing. I paid $3,200 up front for them to publish it. It was such a good story I thought it would fly off the shelves. They told me what format to put it in, which was easy since it was on my computer. I then submitted it to them and they did some editing and suggestions and I accepted all the changes. I had to send it back to them after I proofed the whole book because some of the names had typos in them. They changed it and I accepted their changes. I sent a printout to Tom for him to do a final proofing on. He sent it back and I sent it to Wayne to publish.

When the book came out, Tom said that the next to the last page should have been the last page and the last page should have been the next to the last page. I told him that Wayne wanted more money to change it post-printing. I told him to leave it alone.

He grumbled but I told him I wasn't going to put another penny into it.

I ordered 50 books and was going to have him sign them for book fairs. I even took them to Georgia, when he got out of prison. I insisted he pay me for them. He took ten of them and gave them away. I still made him pay for them. I had paid $8.80 a book for them. He said his son would have to pay me for them and he was an airline pilot, off on a trip. So I got a check in the mail two weeks later for $80.80. I was surprised he kept his word.

When we were finished with the book, he asked me if I wanted to help him with his second book. Scanners had improved and there wouldn't be so many scanner errors. We finished the second book, *The Maracaibo Plot*, in 6 months, going back and forth with proofing and correcting. This one I put on Kindle, and so far, only one person has ordered it in three years.

CHAPTER 16

Living alone isn't for everyone. I enjoyed my time alone reading book after book when I realized that I could actually do something constructive with my reading. I decided to earn a Master's Degree in Education. I really wanted to know how adults learned, because when we would all go to a computer training class at work, as soon as the secretaries got back to their desks, they would call us in Word Processing to ask us how to do what they were just trained to do. So the training just wasn't translating into usable skills. I think the training department was *demonstrating* how to do something, not really teaching the skill to be repeatable at their desk.

One of the most important things I learned was that if you do not use a skill, you lose it. Conversely, if you think about the bad times in your life, reliving them over and over again, that memory becomes stronger. One way I found to stop thinking about my bad childhood was to write about it. I've written it down in this book, so now I can stop thinking about it.

I've replaced those memories with ways to teach adults how to learn new skills. I'm getting involved with adult literacy so others can learn the wonder of reading a good novel. Or even how to read a menu. Can you imagine trying to function without knowing how to read?

I've learned many things just by reading the manual. I once rebuilt the carburetor of my motorcycle just by reading the manual. It's amazing what you can do if you can read.

I sailed through my Masters of Education with a 4.0, *cumma sum laude* (with highest praise). My diploma came with a gold braided tassel which stands for cumma sum laude. So I finally got the praise I was looking for as a child. Furthering your education is a very good way to get that satisfaction you are looking for.

CHAPTER 17

After receiving my Master's Degree, I decided to put an ad on match.com. I thought I would just start dating again. But the first man I met, Fred, was a professional musician and a retired teacher. The first time I kissed him, I knew it was for real. Maybe it was just that I hadn't been kissed in so long. Well, whatever it was, I finally got that divorce from my first husband, and after being a couple for two years, Fred and I finally got married. I love him and I respect him. I think there was a real lack of respect in my first marriage. I was working and going to school, and George was going off to foreign countries and then bike riding with his friends on his off time. The last five years we were together wasn't much of a marriage

But now I have a renewed interest in pleasing someone just because I love him. He does a lot for me, too.

We're working together to get the mortgage paid off early, so that when I retire at 70, maybe we can do some traveling. Fred has been to every state except for Hawaii and Alaska. And he doesn't want to go to Alaska. I told him I don't have any interest in going to Hawaii because it is so expensive. But that I do want to go to Alaska and see the Glaciers. So I guess we'll just have to go to both.

It wasn't always love and joy with Fred. Sometime after our first year, my doctor tried me on a newer type of anti-depressant. I would yell at Fred over little things, and I even moved out to my own apartment near my work. But Fred was persistent. He would call me up and ask if he could come over, and he would stay the night. After a year I moved back in with Fred.

But I was still on the new medication. I would wake up crying, asking Fred if he had a gun. Both of us knew that I needed help in a big way. I called my doctor, but she was out of the country for a month. I knew I couldn't wait that long. I actually found a place where I purchased a small revolver – a .38 special. I also bought hollow-point bullets. I told the sales man, "No, I don't need any practice bullets." I carried that gun with me everywhere for the next two weeks. Then one night when Fred was at a music gig, I loaded the gun for the first time. It was heavy with all that lead loaded in the gun. I closed up the gun chamber and decided this was so dangerous. I hurried to unload the gun and put the bullets back in the box. I put the gun and bullets and sales receipt in my tote bag that went everywhere with me. I put the tote bag in the back seat of my car.

Then I emailed Fred and told him I needed him to take me to the hospital. I called my doctor's office and asked the nurse which hospital they recommended. They said to go to Research Medical Center and my doctor's partner would take care of following me there. We drove to Research Medical Center and I admitted myself voluntarily. My doctor's partner would see to it that I would be put back on the regular medicine that worked so well in the past.

I told Fred to return the gun and bullets to the store, whose address was on the sales receipt.

I spent two weeks at Research Medical Center. I decided while I was there I should try to eat only the leanest items on the menu and lose a few pounds. I was active in the basketball games as well. After the two weeks, I went down two jean sizes. When I was discharged I was picked up by Fred and we've been lovey-dovey ever since. I don't shout at him anymore and I have my happiness back.

CHAPTER 18

Jane is now 16 and has grown into a beautiful young lady. All her friends are sons and daughters of people that Karen knows. It's a very close-knit group. Jane often goes on a road trip with one of the families. She's getting to travel even though Karen doesn't have the money to take her.

In the summer, Karen and Jane go to see George, my first husband, and they work for him for a few weeks. They take a bus to where his next job is going to be, and then they travel with him from job to job. George's job is to scrub the paint on self-storage unit doors and then spray them with anti-rusting fluid. The better he scrubs, the better the fluid sticks to the doors. He gets as many of these jobs as he wants. His boss lines them up for him and all he has to do is show up and do the work. He doesn't have to talk to anyone. They are expecting him when he arrives. He pays Karen and Jane to do the scrubbing, according to how much work they do. He deducts for food and lodging. So depending on how much they eat, they could come back home with enough for the next several months.

Karen also has glass figurines that she sells at festivals. She has an arrangement with a glass-blower. She just sits on a blanket near a main attraction at a festival and spreads her glassware on the blanket. People come up and look and buy. She doesn't have to do much of anything.

Jane makes bracelets, necklaces and even masks, and sells them at festivals. She gets the beads and clasps at Walmart. The individual pieces are very cheap, but she makes them so beautiful. For Mother's Day she gave me a rock with shiny turquoise in it, called it a peacock, and put it in a miniature cage. It doesn't look like a peacock, but its color is reminiscent of one, and so it makes perfect sense that she calls it a peacock in a cage. I love it and wear it to work often.

CHAPTER 19

I had worked at my job for 13 years when they offered an early retirement incentive for those of a certain age and length of service. I was the only one to accept. I got a nice amount of money and decided to move to Georgia. I didn't want to see another Kentucky Winter.

Before I even left, I had picked out and given a deposit for a nice apartment in a gated community. I had also arranged for an interview at a big law firm. I had signed a contract for a moving company to move my stuff, all without talking to Fred about it. The night before I was to leave, I told him I was moving to Georgia. He didn't argue much about it. I wished he had, because the three months I spent in Georgia were not much fun.

The car trip was fine. I used my Garmin GPS and took three days to get down there. I liked living on my own again, but I didn't get the job I interviewed for. Every day I filled out an application for a job online. I just could not get a job. I had enough money for a few months, but without a job I had no insurance for my medications. I went through withdrawal from my anti-depressant and sleep medication. I hardly slept the first week off my meds. I was a wreck.

My whole intestinal system was terribly upset. I had diarrhea several times every day. I kept taking Imodium AD every day. When I ran out of my diabetes meds I started urinating every 10 minutes. After several weeks of this I decided to ask the nearby pharmacy how much each medication would be without insurance. My anti-depressants were $1100 a month. My sleep medication was only $24, so I renewed that. My diabetes meds were only $30, so I renewed that. My blood-pressure medication was only $14, so I got those renewed. My most important medication, my anti-depressant, was more than I wanted to spend, so I started taking St. John's Wart. It didn't help at all. I just tried to live without it.

After the three months were over, I asked Fred if it was okay to come home and live as husband and wife again. He said, "Sure!"

For the trip home I decided to throw out everything I could live without and I just packed the car instead of using a moving service. This time I only took two days to get home. The first day I stopped early because the rain made it get dark early, and I don't like driving in the dark. The next day I got up early and took advantage of the free breakfast at the hotel. Then I drove from 8 a.m. to 5 p.m., only stopping to use the bathroom and get gas. I didn't stop to eat. I drank Ensure for an entire day whenever I got hungry.

Fred forgave me and we've been living happily ever after.

CHAPTER 20

I still needed to get another job. I worked at a small branch of a large accounting firm for a total of three months. I left because I was having high anxiety and deep depression. This caused me to keep making mistakes. I was ashamed of my poor performance. I left suddenly the morning I realized I had made another mistake. I wrote a short letter of resignation and then left.

So I was back to square one. I went out to interviews and filled out on-line applications. I interviewed with several large law firms. Then an old co-worker called me about a new word processing department she was putting together for a law firm. We were to be a centralized Word Processing department for the entire firm. Prior to this San Diego handled most of the WP requests for the firm. But the firm wanted all administrative positions in a centralized location in Louisville. Marketing, Personnel, Accounting, IT, and Word Processing were all in one building. We filled the entire 7th floor of our downtown building. The best part of it was that there were no attorneys in our location. Everything came via email. Dictation, litigation documents, memos, letters – everything.

After taking their tests for MS Word, Excel and Power Point, interviewing with several of their people across the country via video conference, and passing their background check, I was welcomed into the firm. The word processors in San Diego would be let go in three months' time, all but one, who would be a satellite word processor in San Diego. San Diego is a large branch office, so it will be nice for them to have a word processor there.

CHAPTER 21

I'd say that I've been through a lot in my life. What I've written about only skims the edges, but the flavor of most phases of my life are represented. As a child all my material needs were met. As a young adult, I had joy and love without material wealth. Now, as I approach my 62nd birthday, I can finally say that I have it all – joy and love, and enough resources to make me happy. If I could put my life on hold, this is the period of my life that I would choose to stay in.

But things don't stay the same. I would say that I have the insight and perception to be able to take whatever comes next. I'm sure it will be another outstanding adventure.

I want to stress the point that by helping others with their needs, you can stop thinking about a terrible childhood. But most of all, before you can help someone else, you must help yourself first. Talk to a psychologist about your past. Also, it wouldn't hurt to talk to a psychiatrist to see if you can get a diagnosis, such as Post Traumatic Stress Syndrome, or Bi-Polar Disorder, or Severe Depression. Those things can be treated with medication. I am amazed at how the right medication can help me tremendously, and another similar medication made me psychotic. Medicine is not an exact science. Sometimes they have to try you on different medications, and sometimes it takes three weeks to take effect. It's very frustrating to the patient. But once you find what works, stick with it. Some medication manufacturers even have foundations that will pay for your meds for a year. If you google the medication, you can usually find the foundation that will help pay for your meds.

I would be very interested to hear from my readers about how they are coping with their abusive childhood, successfully or not. Maybe we can create a book of case studies, names changed, of course. Here's what I would like to know:

1. How old are you?
2. What is the earliest memory of abuse?
3. Are you living alone?
4. Are you in a stable relationship?
5. Are you in a safe place?
6. Have you regularly seen a psychologist?
7. Have you regularly seen a psychiatrist?
8. Are you taking medications?
9. Are your meds working for you?
10. How do you pay for your meds (insurance, Medicaid, Medicare, self-pay)
11. What is the most important goal you want to achieve in the next 12 months?

Feel free to correspond with me at c/o Debra Baker, 5612 N. Smalley, Kansas City, MO 64119.

Printed in the United States
By Bookmasters